The
Delightful
World

of

Undersea
Majesty

Printed in the United States of America

First Printing, 2016

Illustrated by: Savana Ellison

The fish are watching

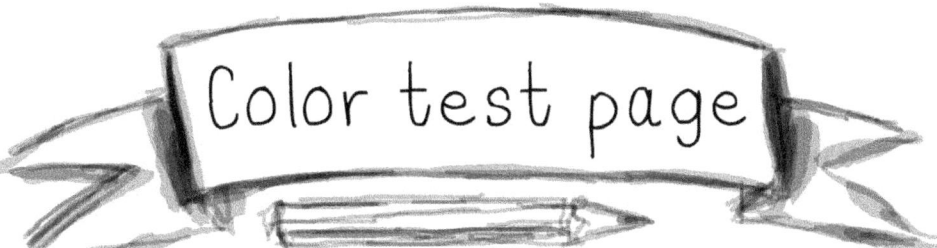

Color test page

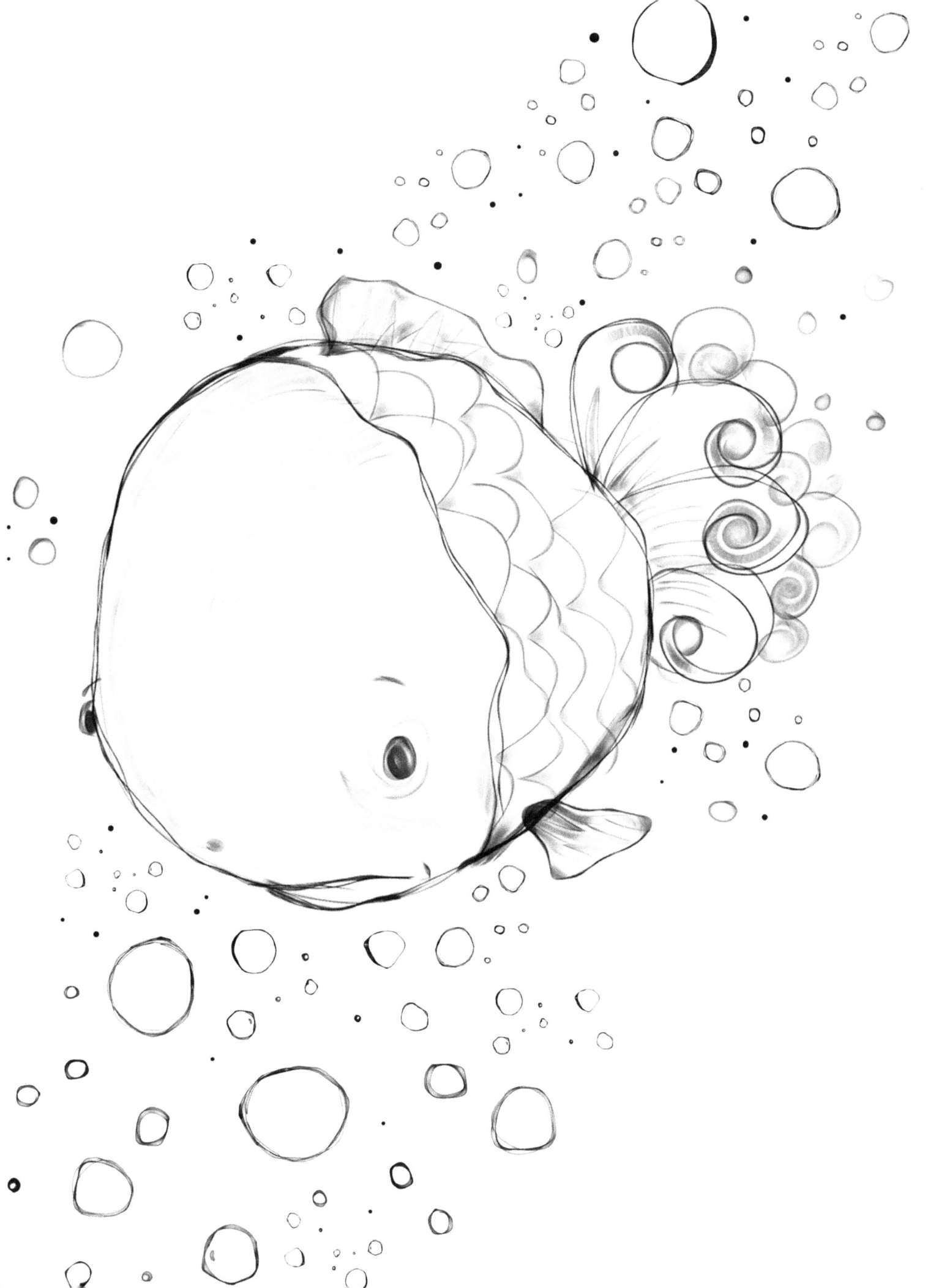

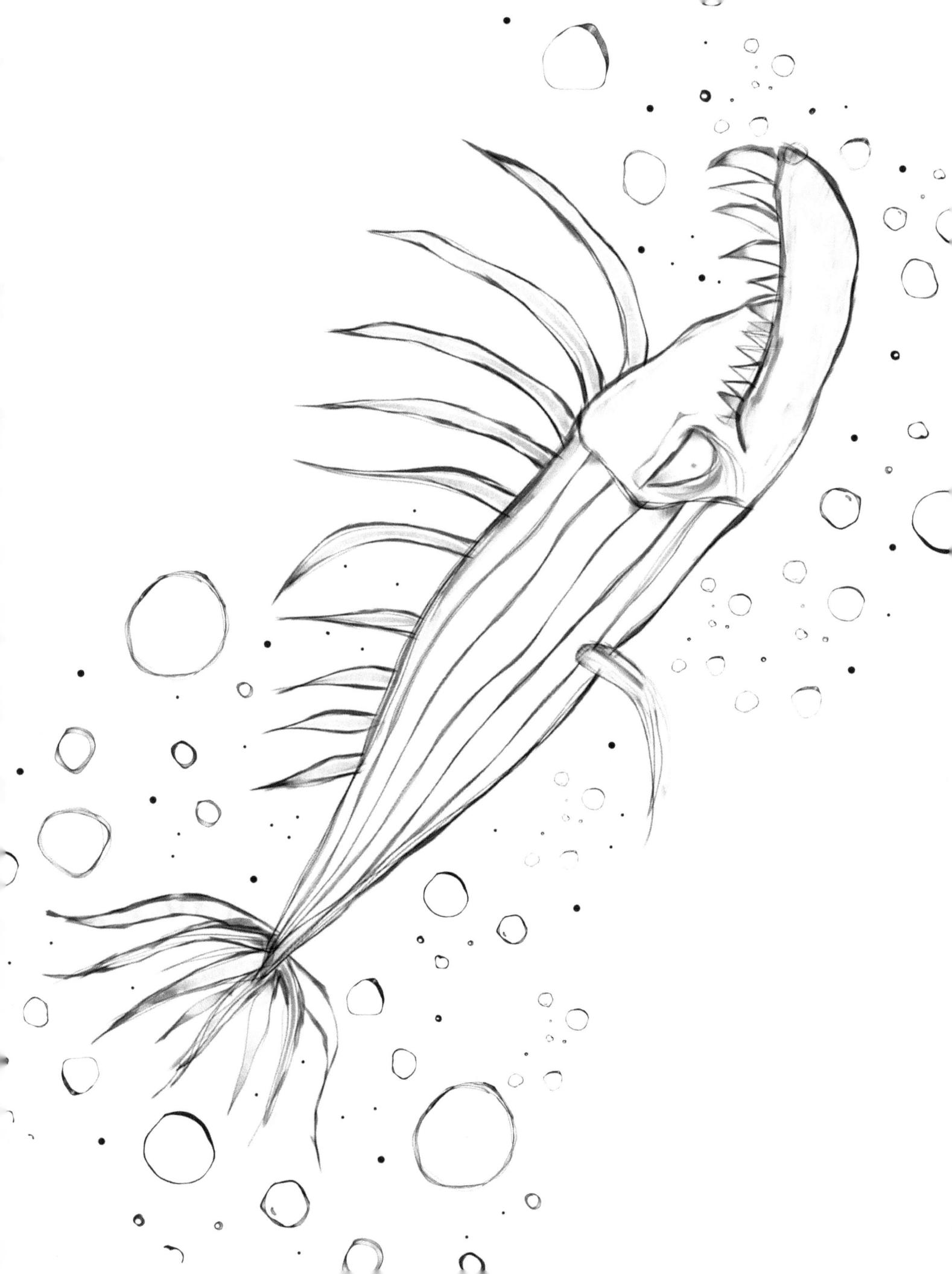

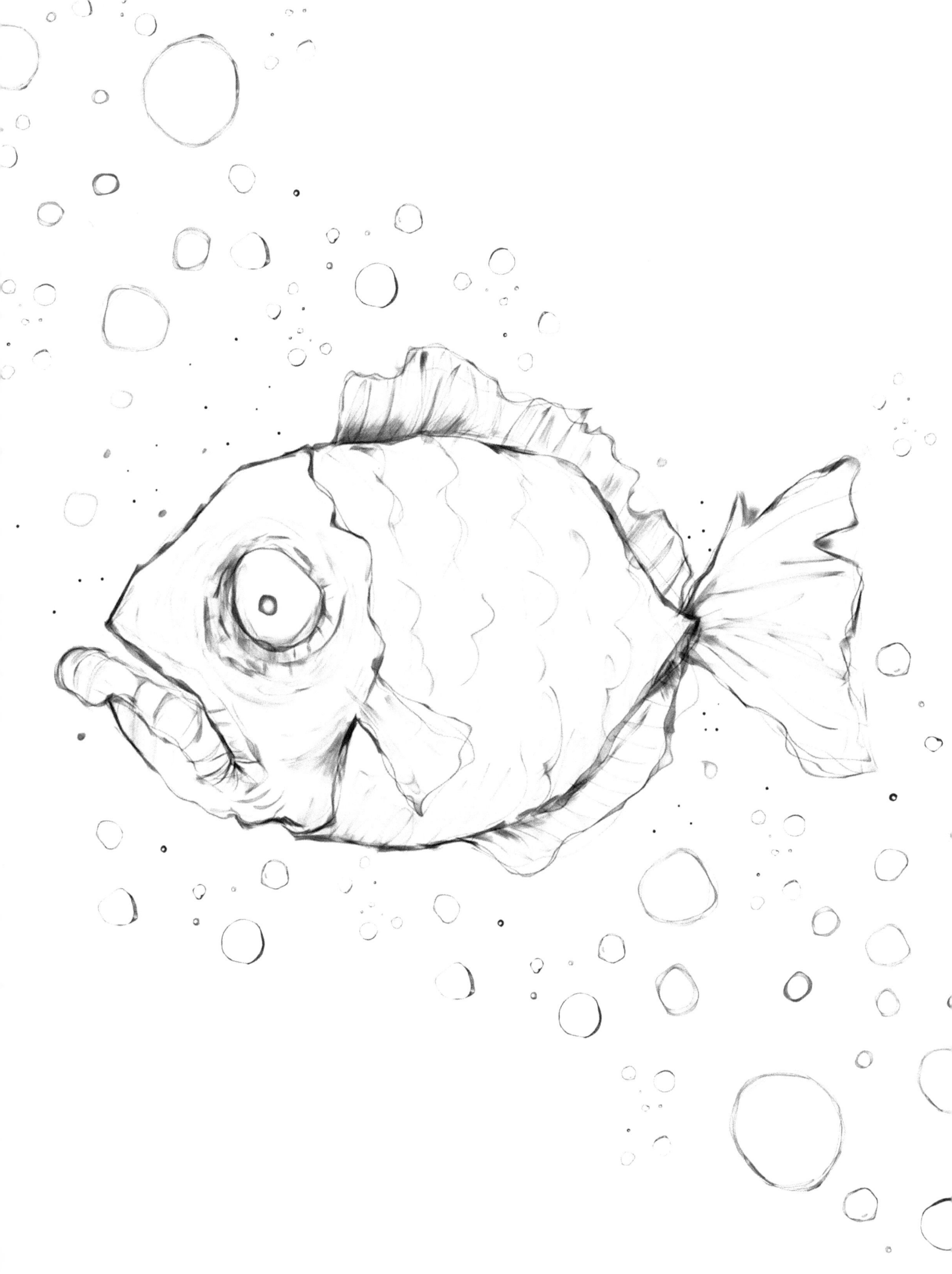

The fish are watching

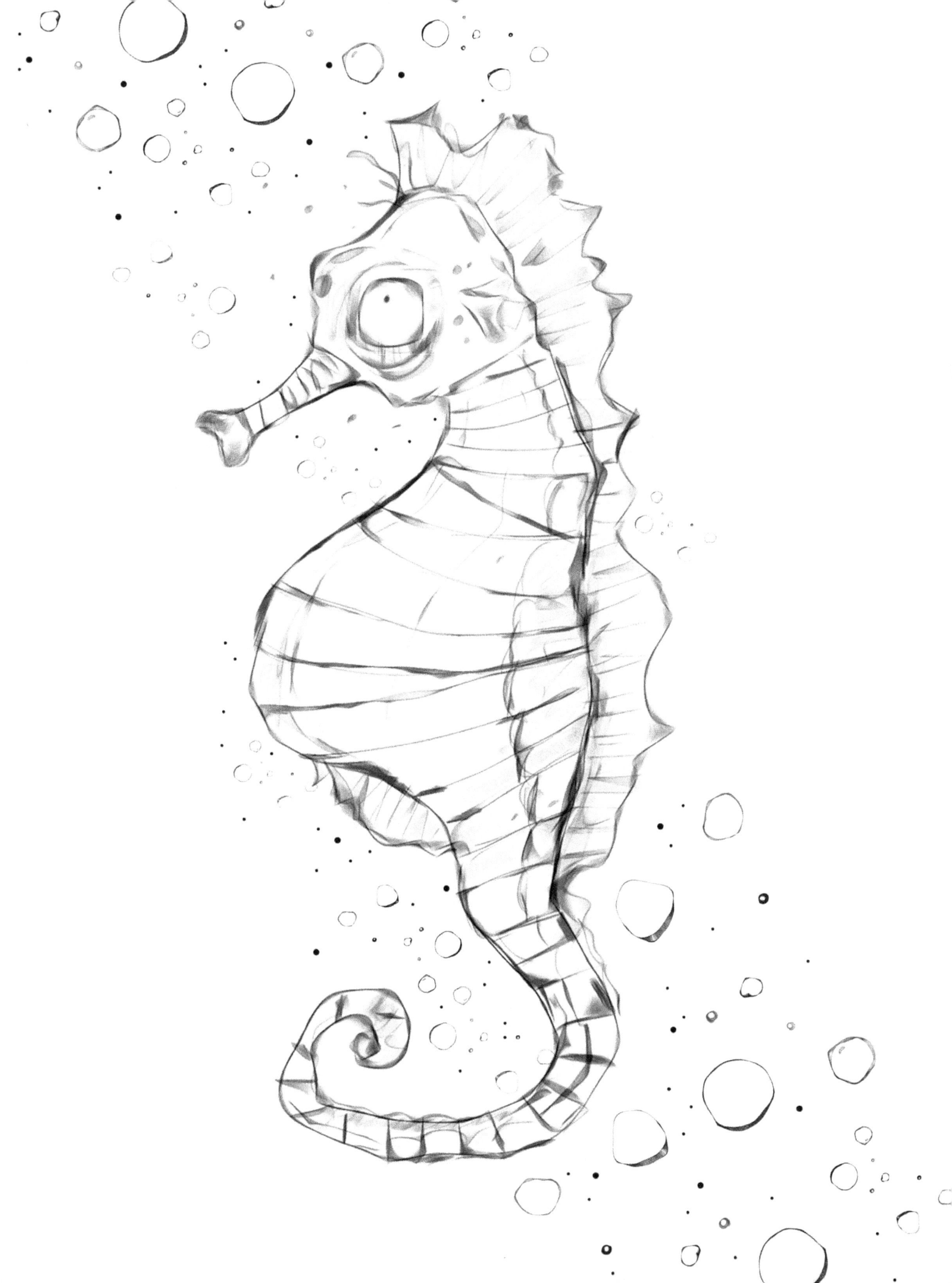

The fish are watching

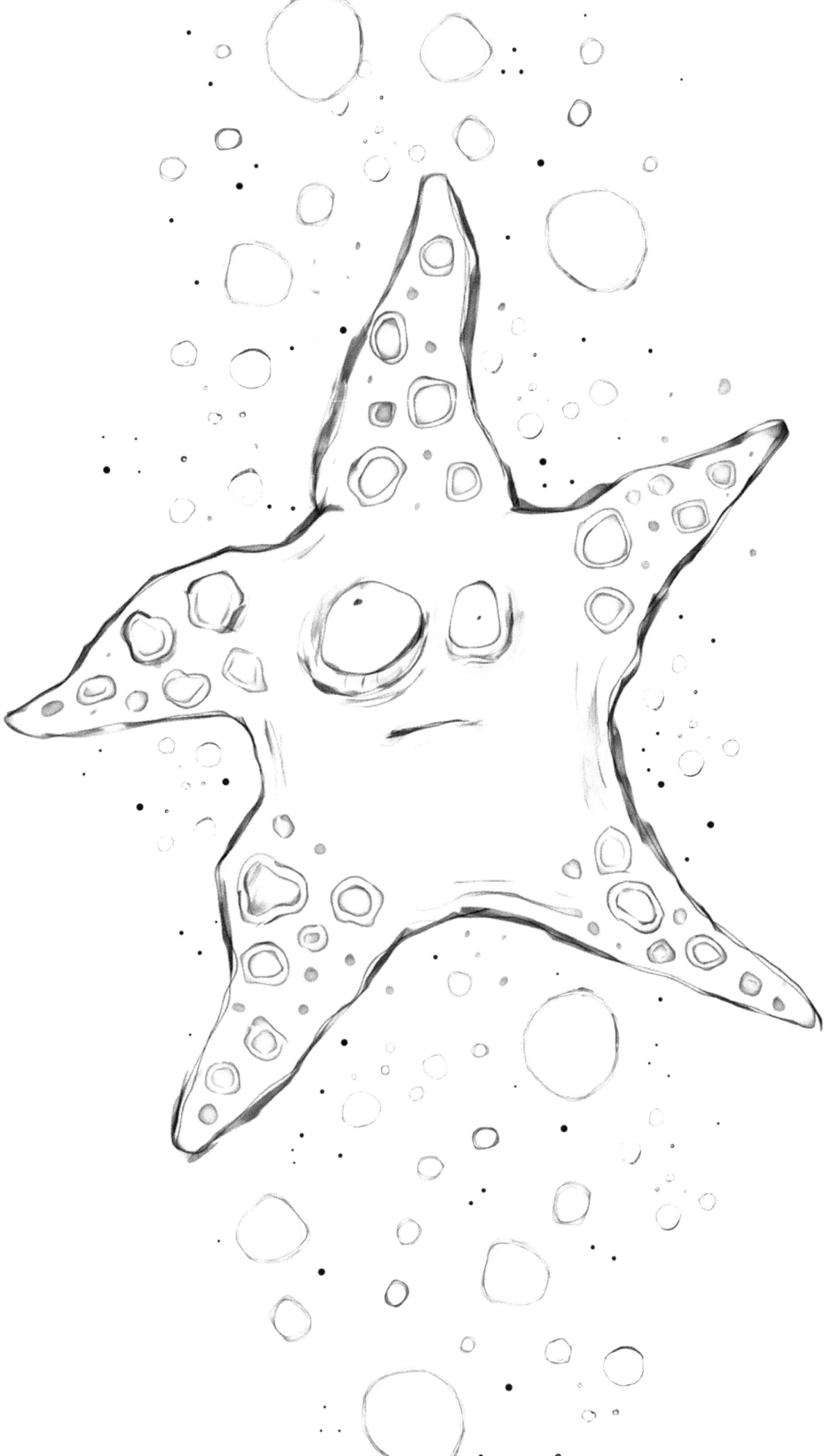

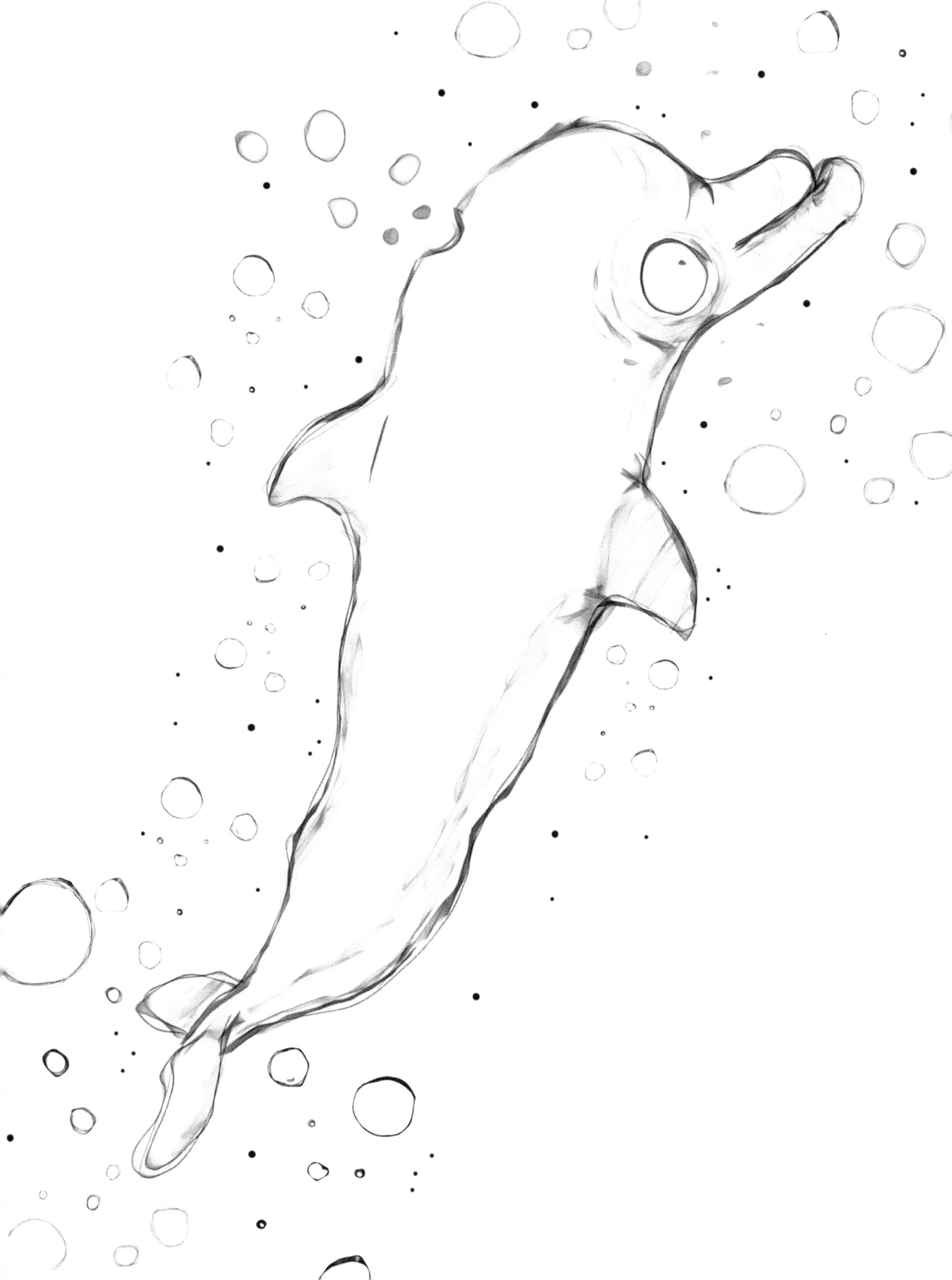

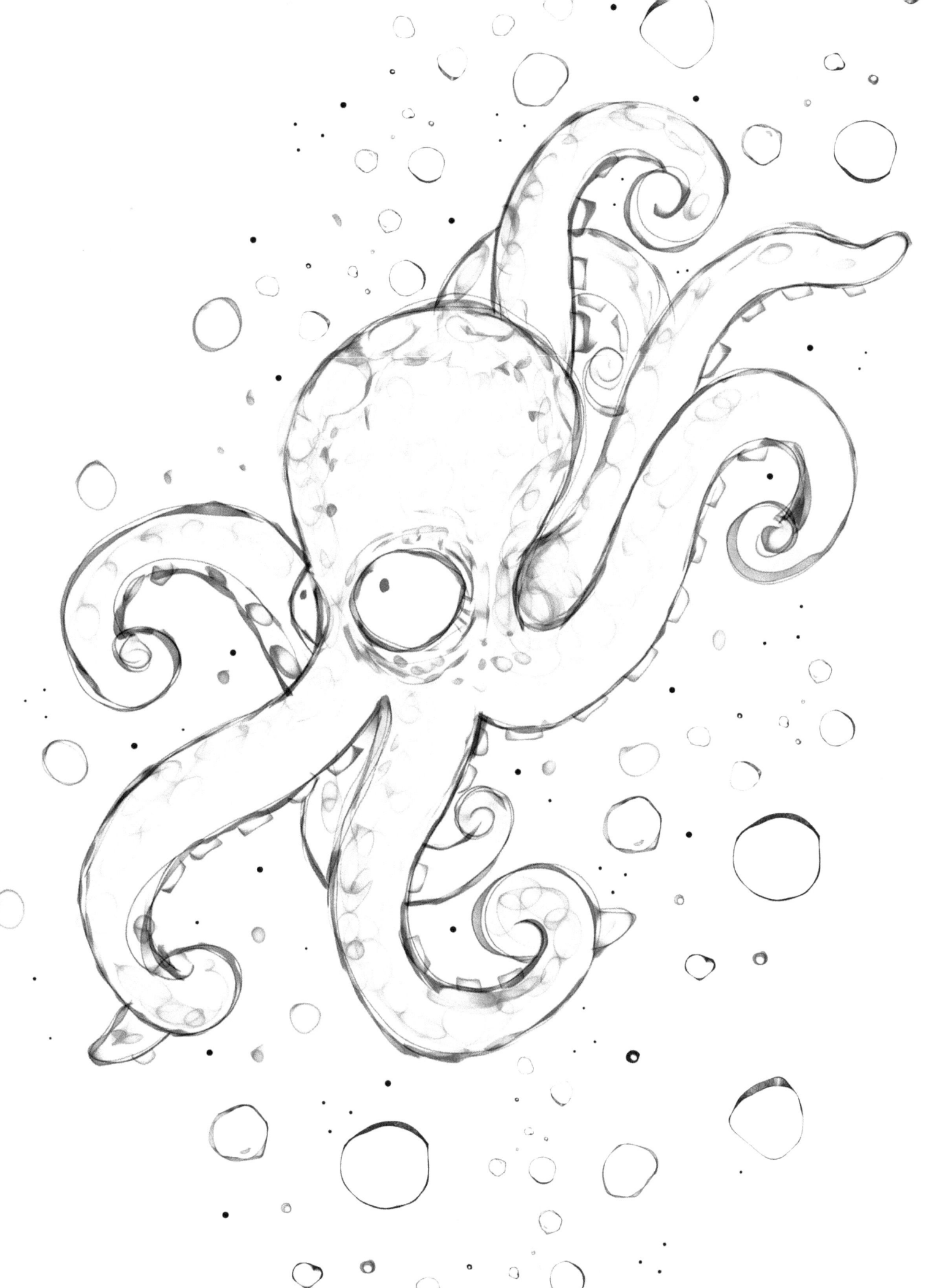

The fish are watching

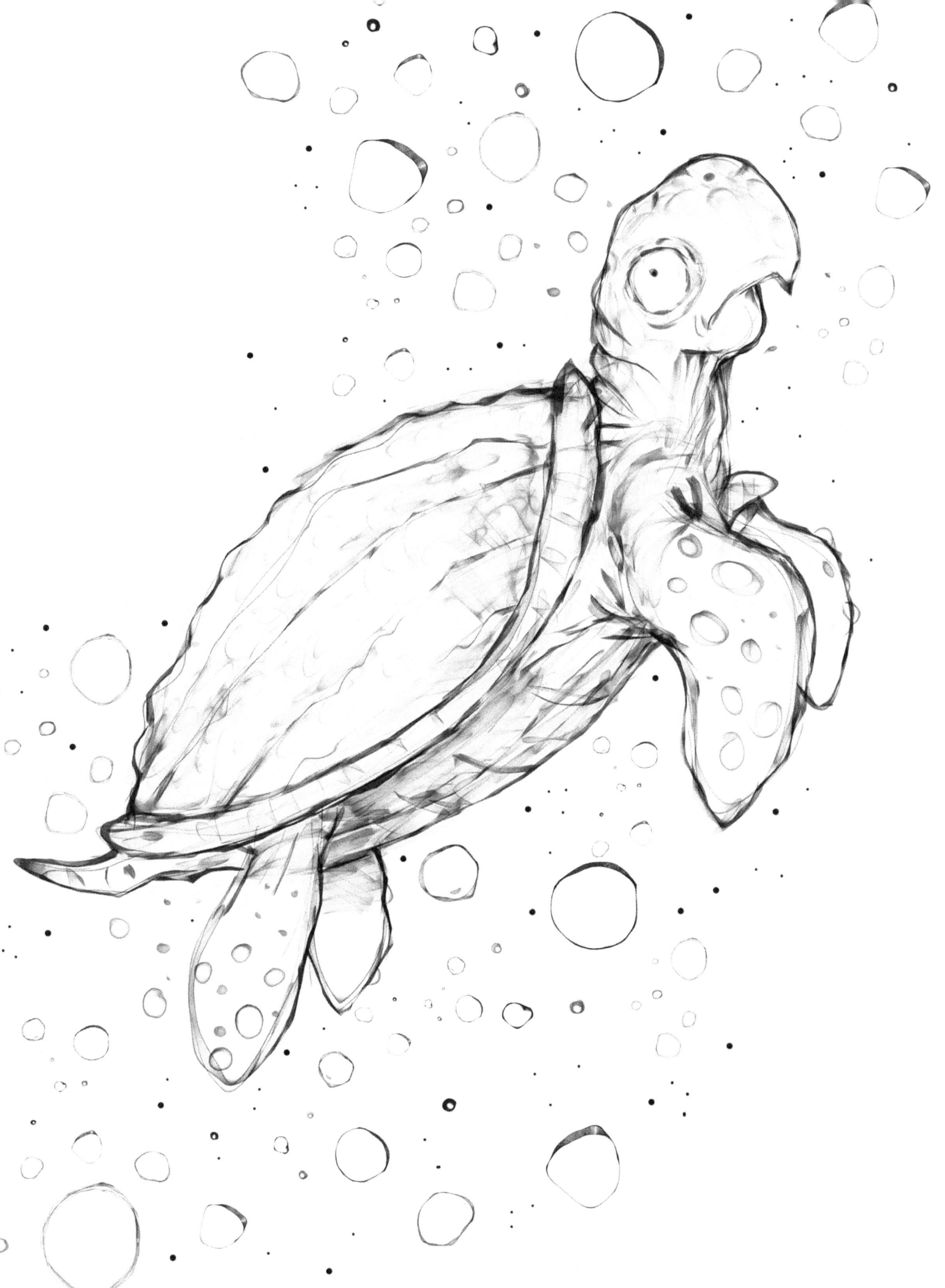

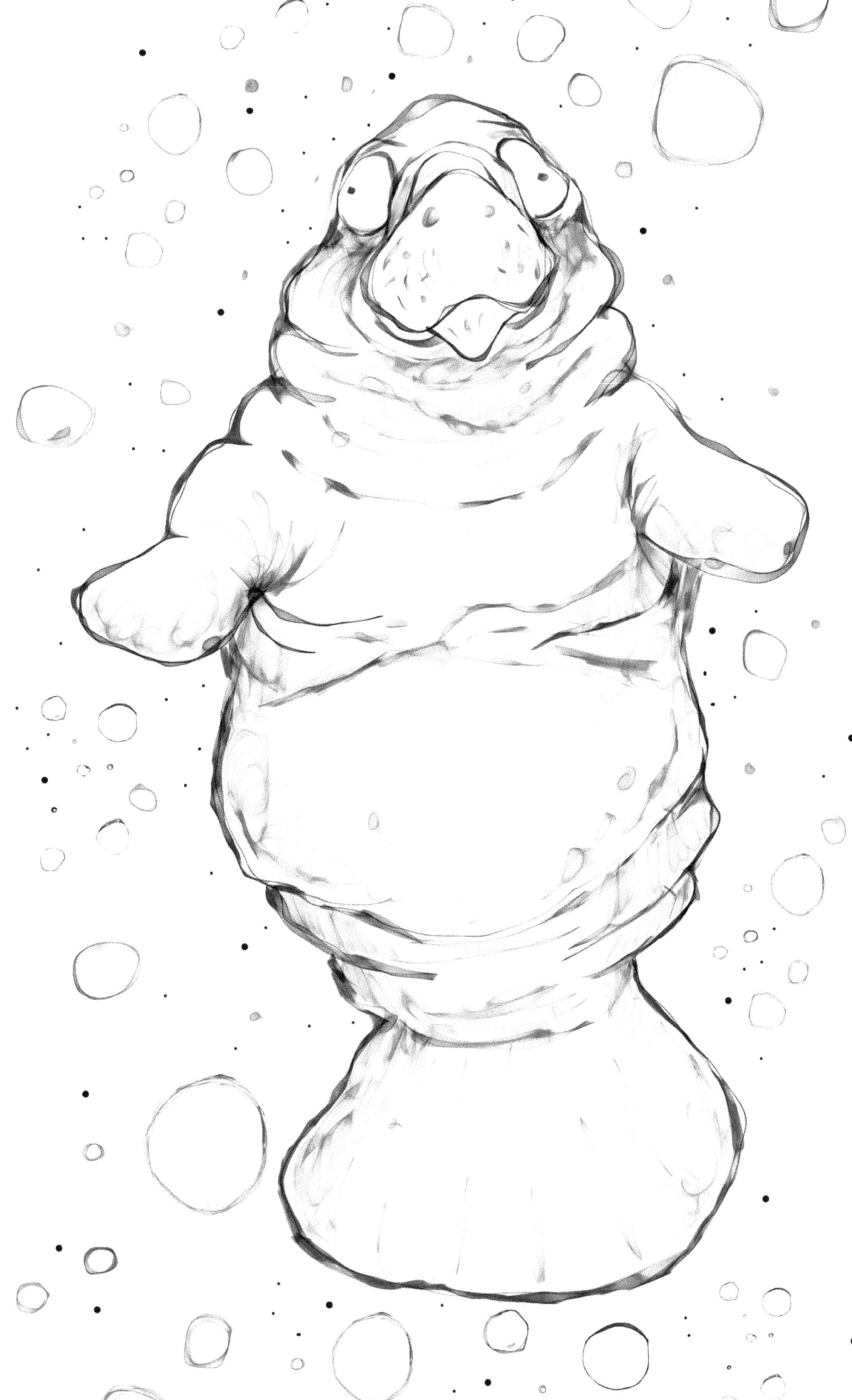

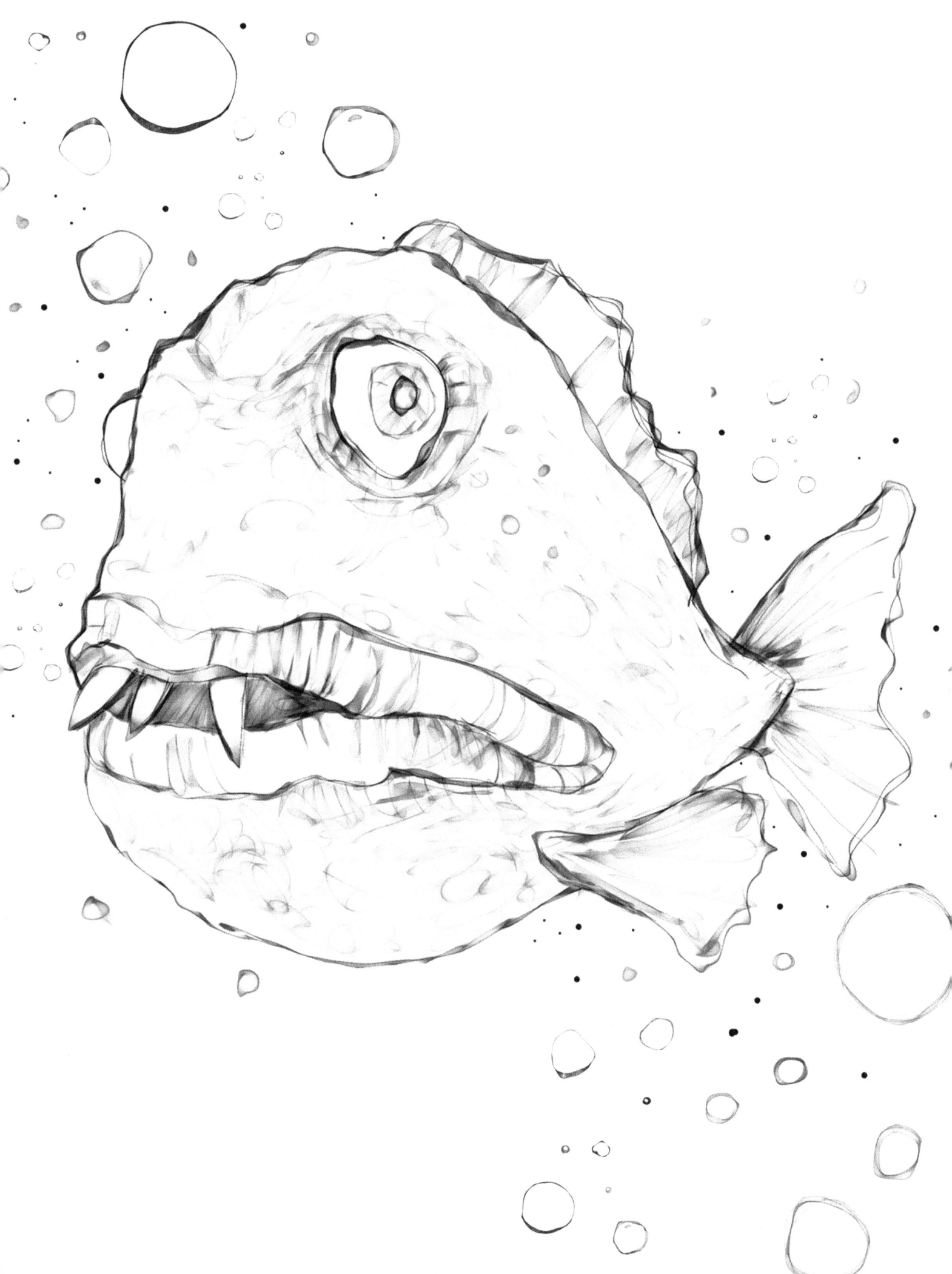

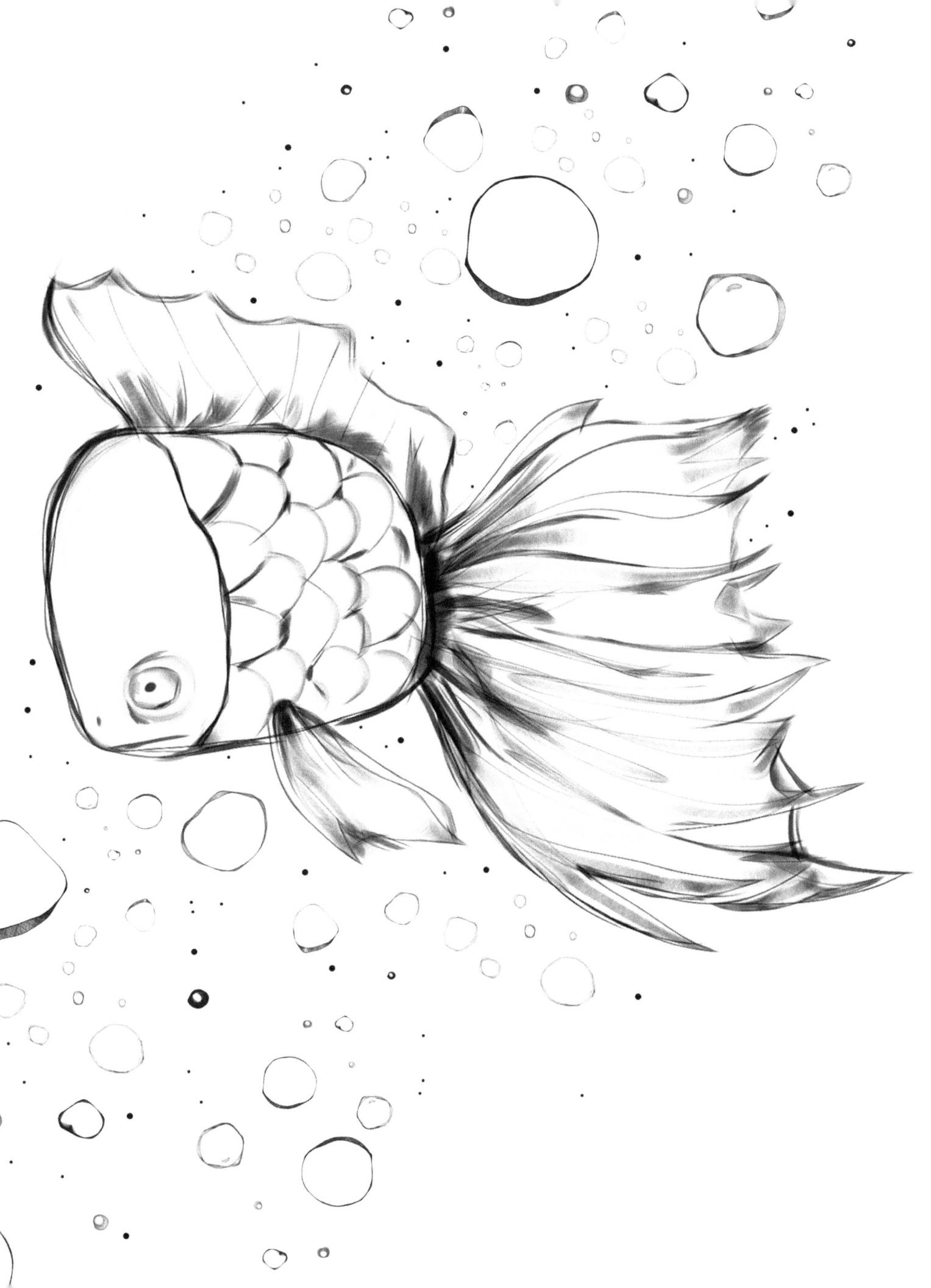

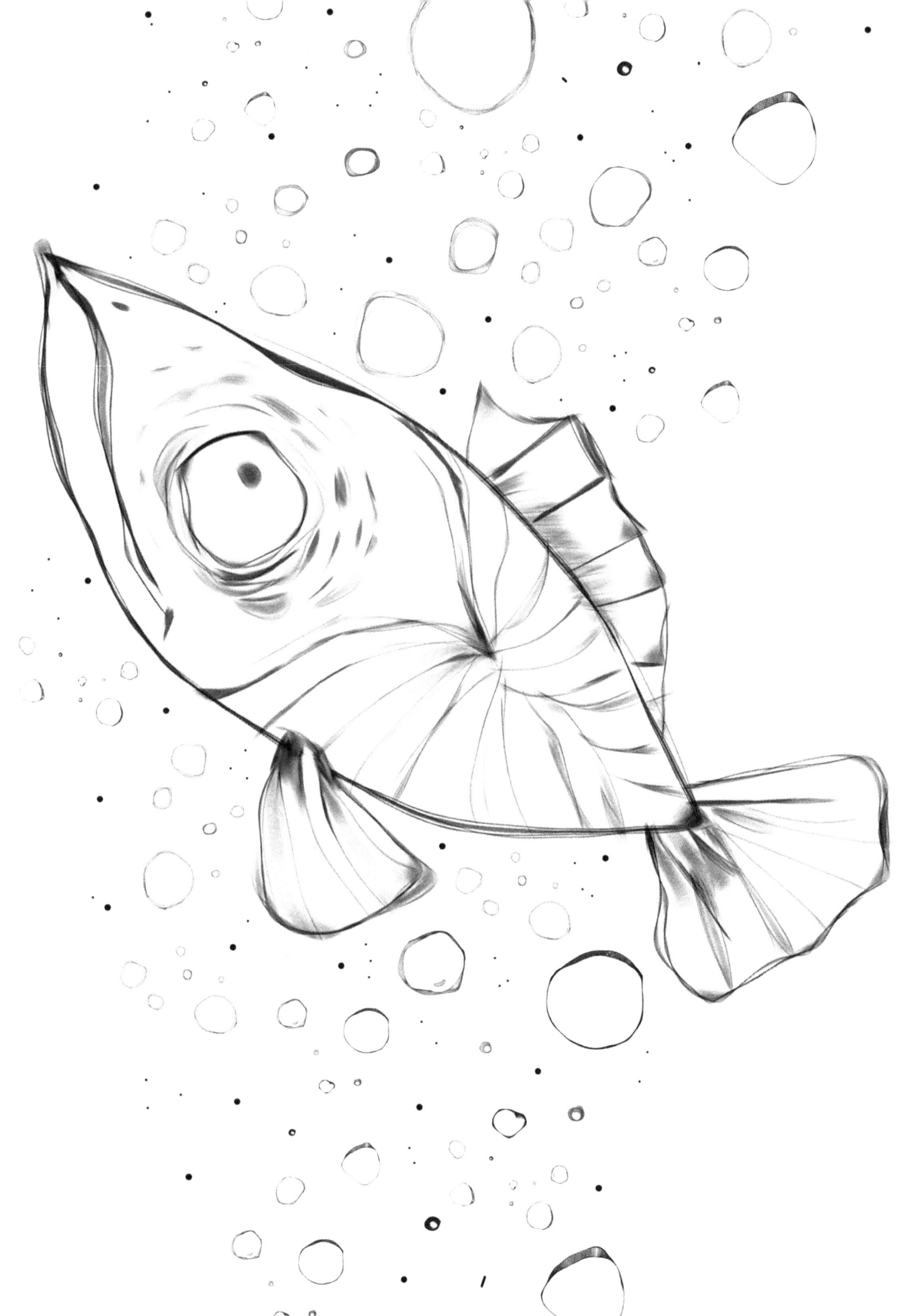

The fish are watching

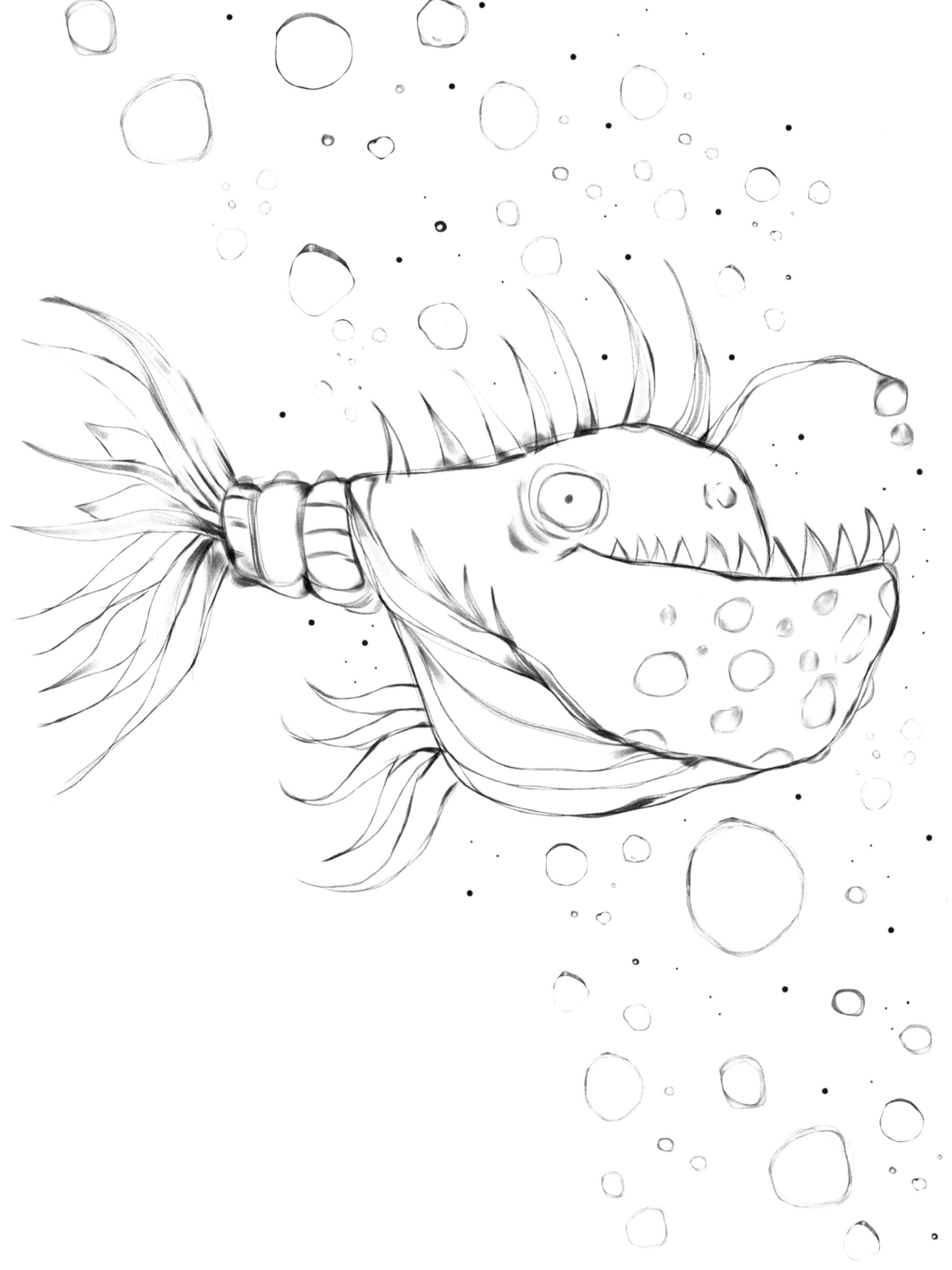

The fish are watching

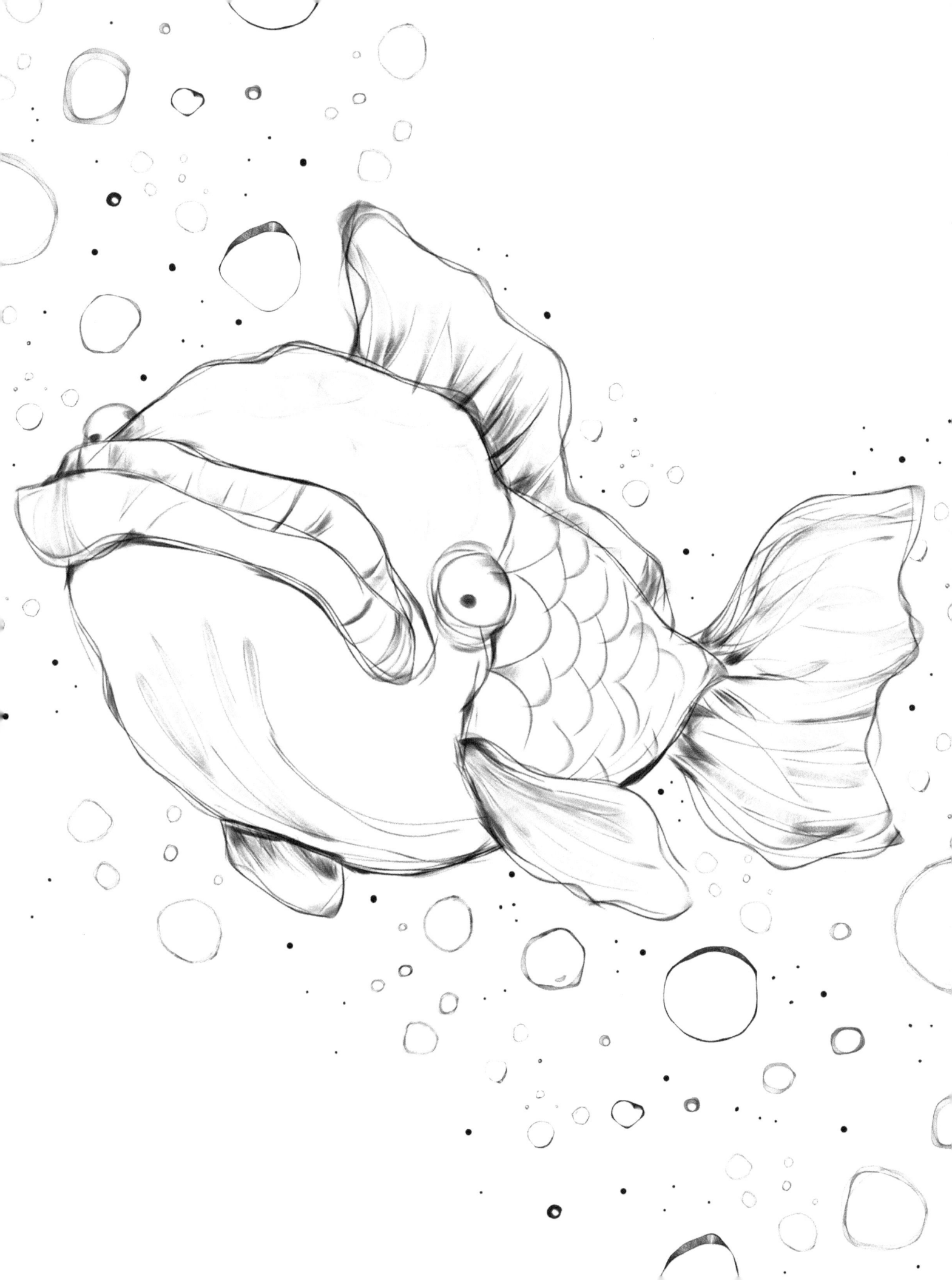

The fish are watching

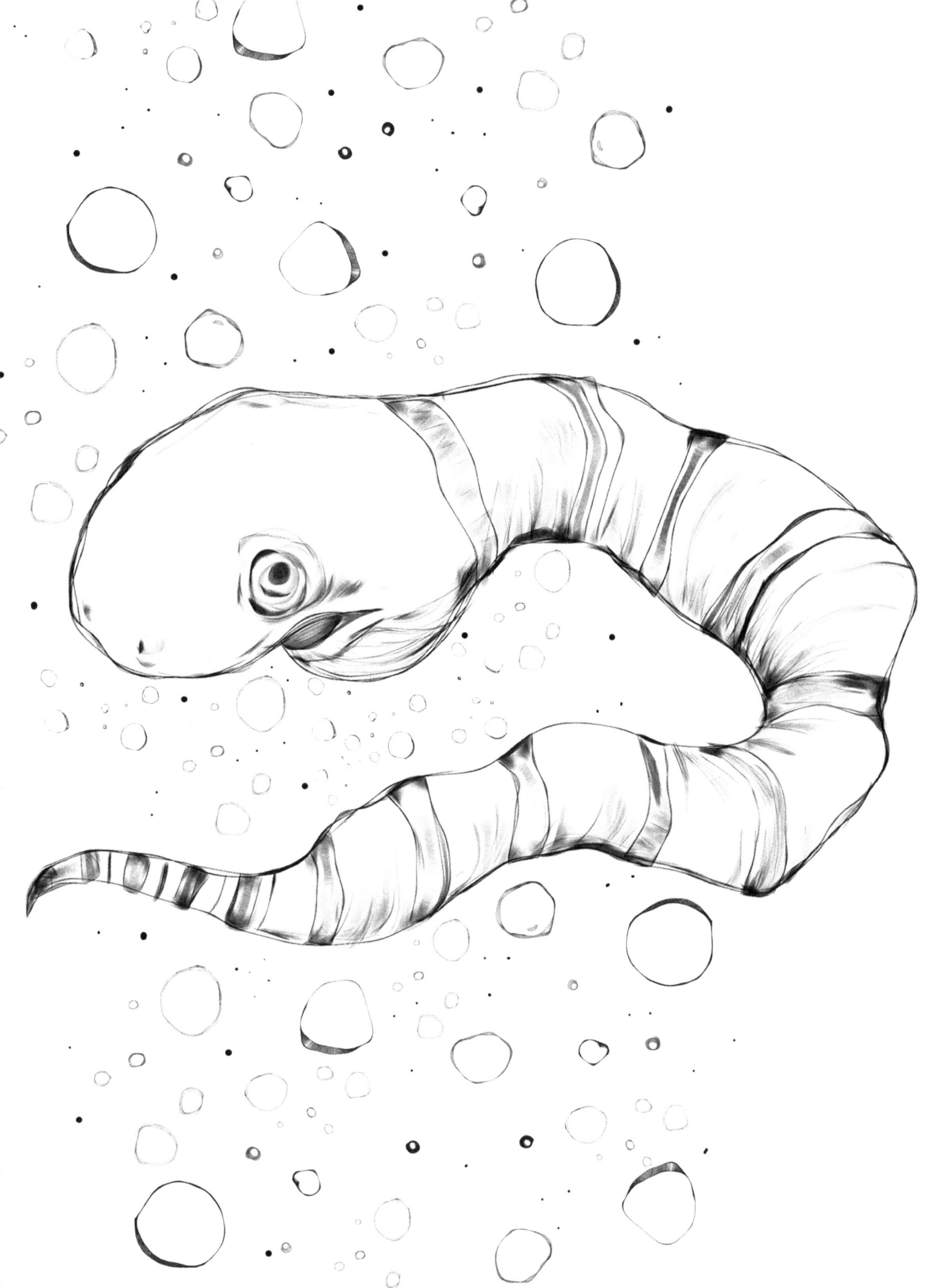

The fish are watching

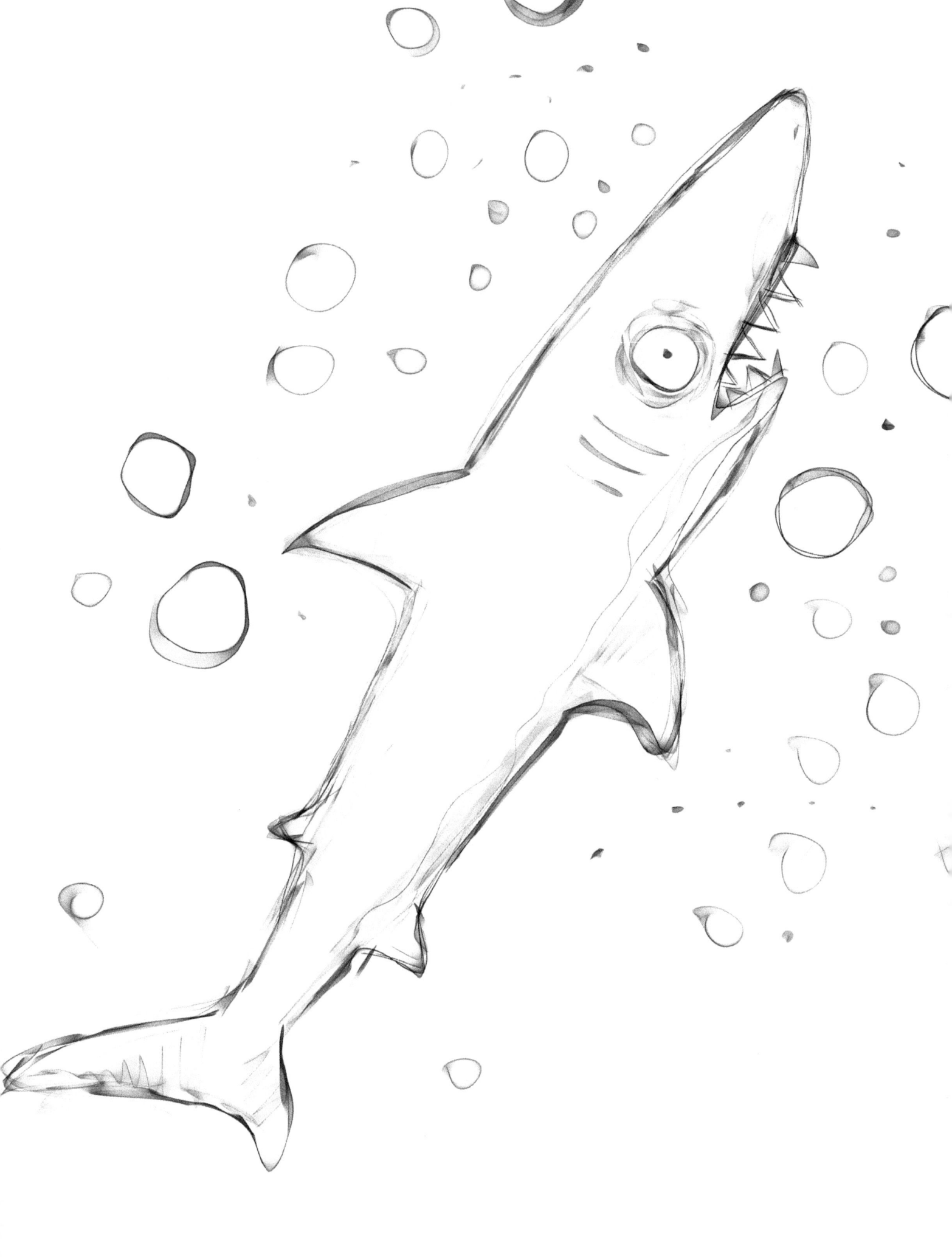

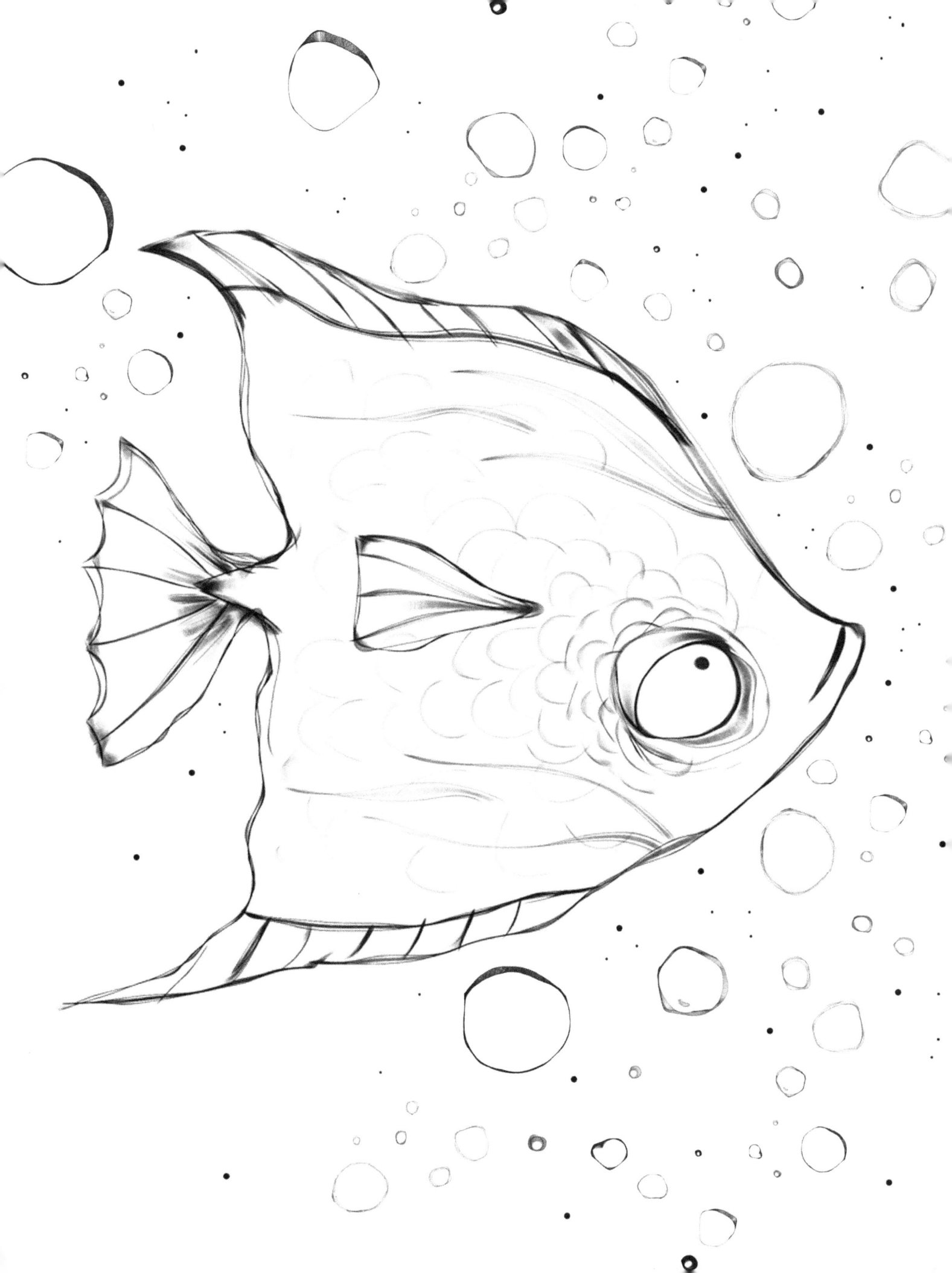

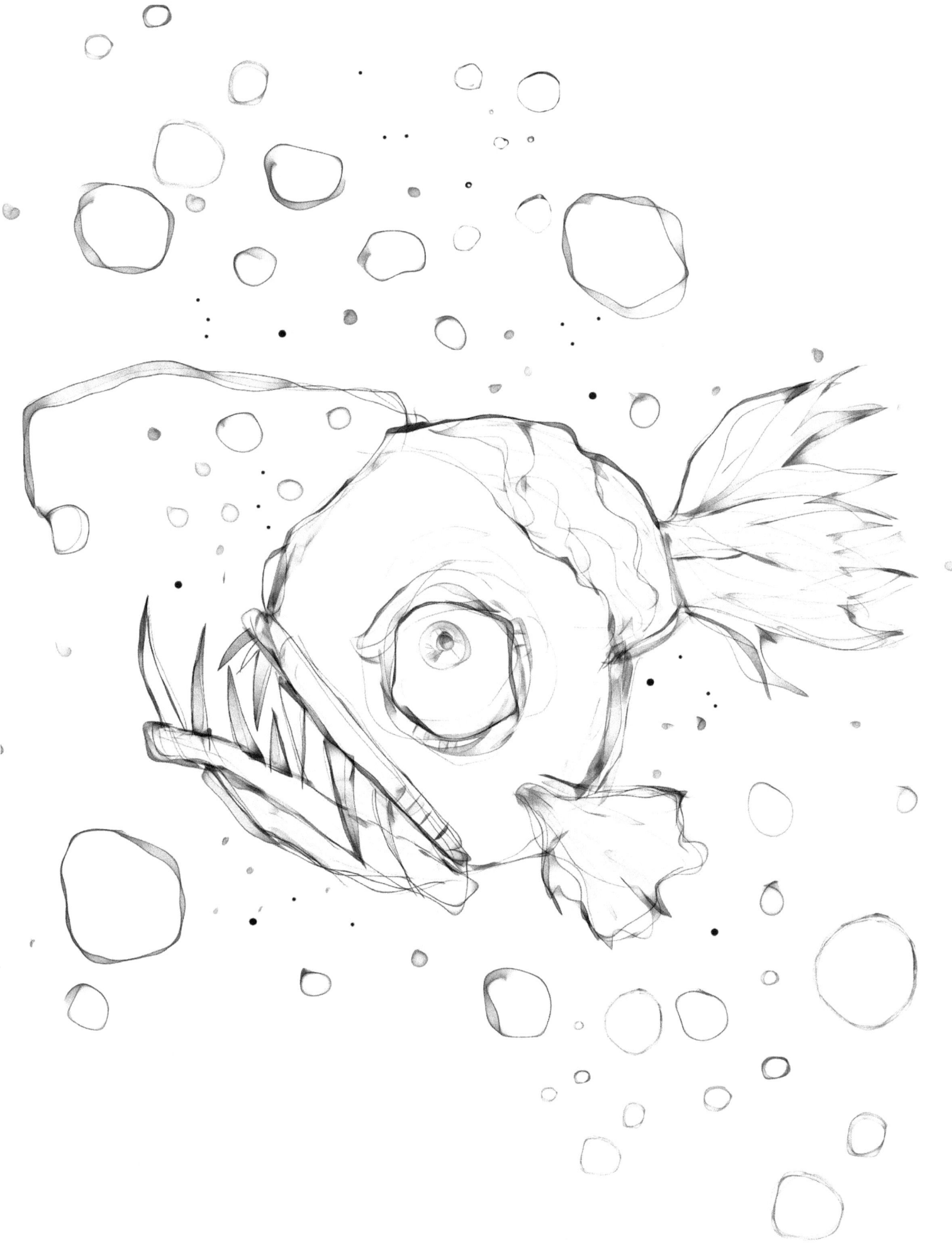

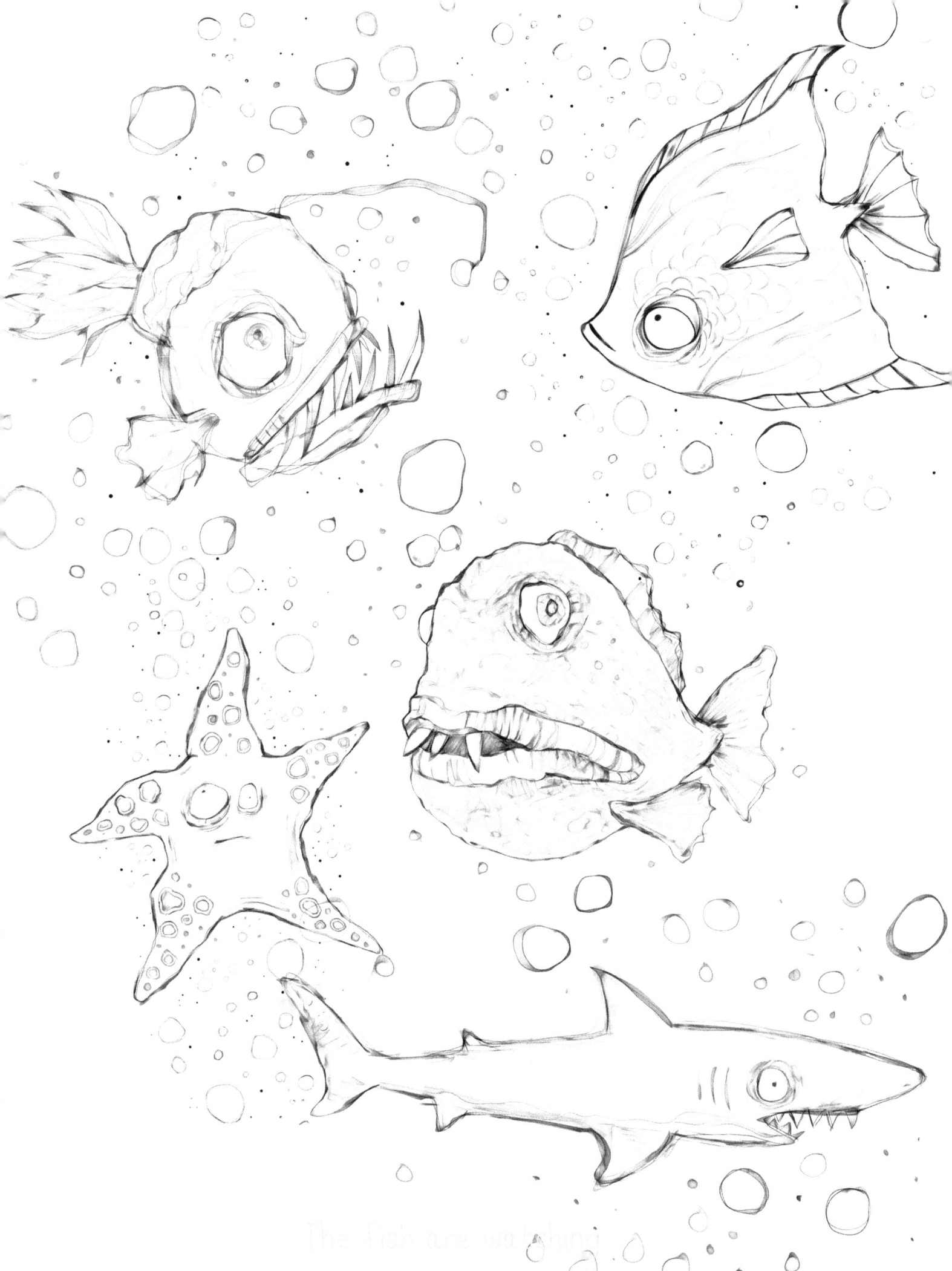

The fish are watching

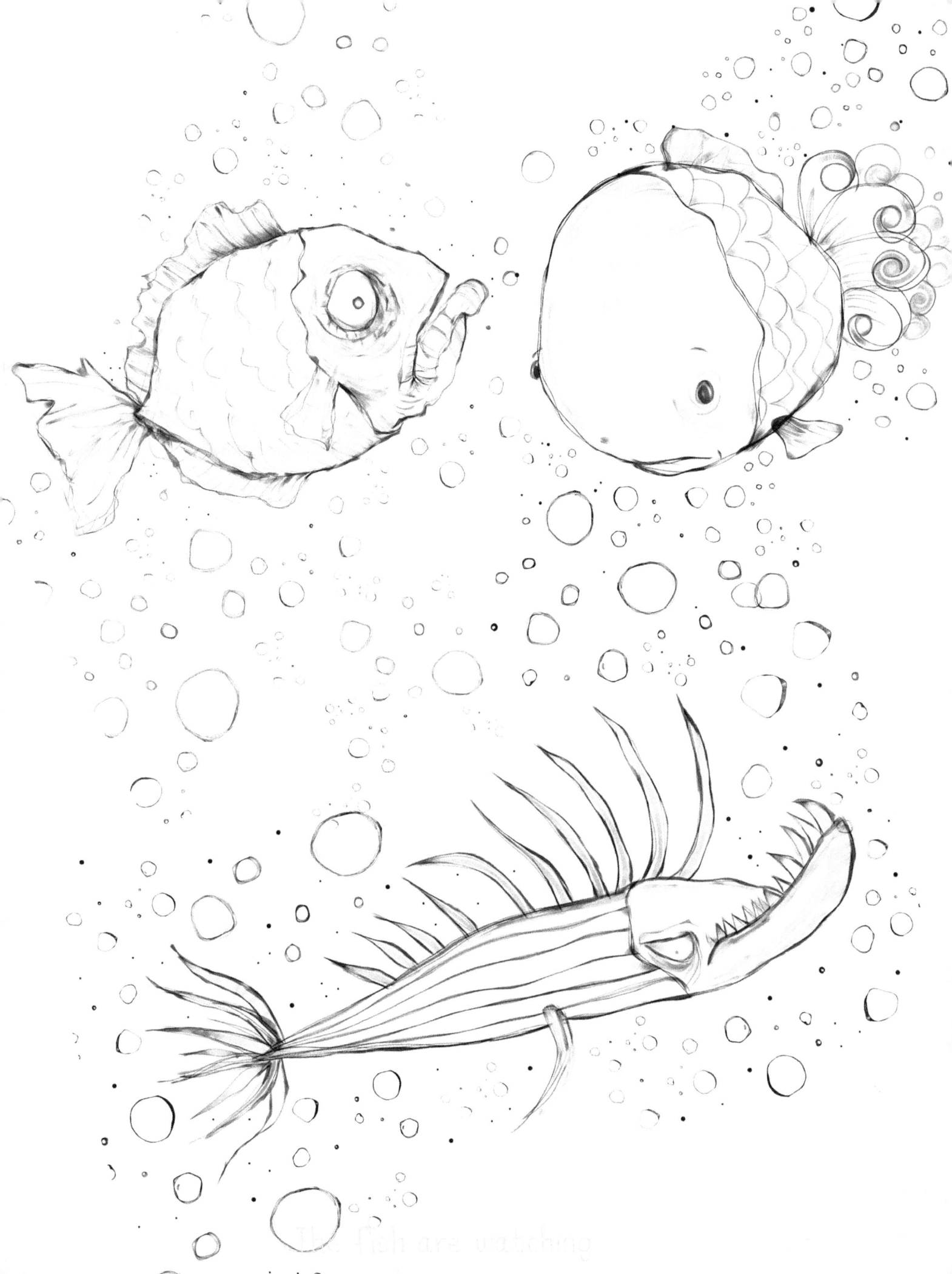